MCR

CELLS

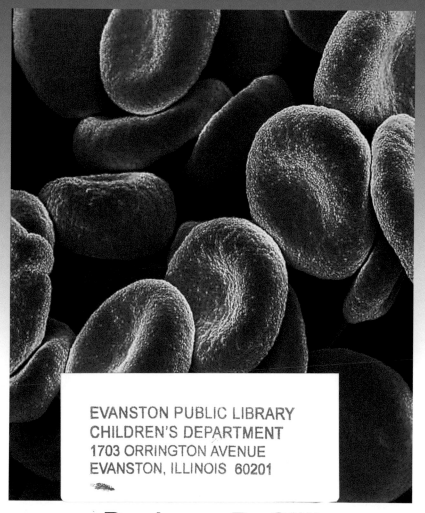

Darlene R. Stille
Contributing author: Carol Ryback

Science consultant: Suzy Gazlay, M.A., science curriculum resource teacher

Gareth Stevens
Publishing

Please visit our web site at: www.garethstevens.com
For a free color catalog describing Gareth Stevens Publishing's list
of high-quality books, call 1-800-542-2595 (USA)
or 1-800-387-3178 (Canada).

Library of Congress Cataloging-in-Publication Data

Stille, Darlene R.
    Cells / Darlene Stille. — North American ed.
       p. cm. — (Gareth Stevens vital science: life science)
    Includes bibliographical references and index.
    ISBN-13: 978-0-8368-8437-1 — ISBN-10: 0-8368-8437-X (lib. bdg.)
    ISBN-13: 978-0-8368-8446-3 — ISBN-10: 0-8368-8446-9 (softcover)
    1. Cells—Juvenile literature.   I. Title.
  QH582.5.S752   2008
  571.6—dc22   2007021474

This edition first published in 2008 by
Gareth Stevens Publishing
A Weekly Reader® Company
1 Reader's Digest Road
Pleasantville, NY 10570-7000 USA

Q2a Media editor: Honor Head
Q2a Media design, illustrations, and image search: Q2a Media
Q2a Media cover design: Q2a Media

Gareth Stevens editor: Carol Ryback
Gareth Stevens art direction: Tammy West
Gareth Stevens graphic designer: Dave Kowalski
Gareth Stevens production: Jessica Yanke
Gareth Stevens science curriculum consultant: Suzy Gazlay, M.A.

Photo credits: t=top, b=bottom, m=middle, l=left, r=right
Photolibrary: / Science Photo Library: half title, 11(tl), 13, 35, 39(b); / Photo Researchers, Inc.: 5,
15(b), 41; / Dr. Gordon Beakes © University of Newcastle upon Tyne, Oxford Scientific Films 8(b),
18(tl); / Science Photolibrary: / 11(tr); / Phototake Inc. 17, 19 (b), 36 (br). Shutterstock: / Marilyn
Barbone 21(b); / Vladimir Mucibabic 40(m), 40(mr). iStockphoto: / Viktor Pryymachuk 43(b).

Every effort has been made to trace the copyright holders for the photos used in this book.
The publisher apologizes, in advance, for any unintentional omissions and would be pleased
to insert the appropriate acknowledgments in any subsequent edition of this publication.

Printed in the United States of America

1 2 3 4 5 6 7 8 9 11 10 09 08 07

Contents

1

What Is a Cell?

Everything alive is made of cells. A cell is the basic building block of all plants and animals. It carries out the life processes of that organsim and is much like its own little factory of life. Sometimes, one cell makes up the entire plant or animal. Other times, the plant or animal is multicellular—it has more than one cell, or even millions of cells or more.

Each cell of any living thing has in common several parts, such as an outer boundary. This outer boundary is called a cell wall in plants and a cell membrane in animals. The main body of a cell contains a gel-like substance called the cytoplasm. Any number of tiny, internal cell parts may float within the cytoplasm. The cytoplasm contains everything that a cell needs to make energy from food, eliminate waste, and carry out all the functions of life.

Similar—but Different

Different kinds of cells appear in different kinds of organisms. Human beings, for example, have about two hundred different kinds of cells. Overall, an adult human can have as many as ten trillion cells.

Cells that make up the animals and plants we commonly see contain a structure called the nucleus.

4

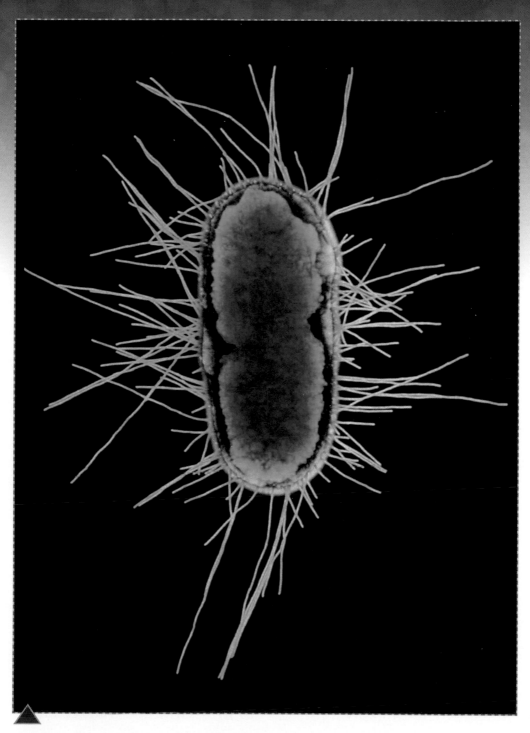

Single cells, such as this bacterium, can
only be seen through a powerful microscope.

The nucleus functions as the command center of the cell. Cells that have a nucleus are called eukaryotic cells.

The nucleus contains copies of that organism's genetic material, or genes. Genes are made of a chemical called DNA (deoxyribonucleic acid). The DNA carries a code for all the workings of a cell. Genes "tell" the cell how to develop and how to function.

The cytoplasm of most cells contains other tiny parts called organelles. Each organelle is specialized to perform a specific function in the life processes of a cell.

Bacteria are single-celled organisms. They are found everywhere. Some bacteria cause disease, but many do not. Bacteria are very simple cells. They do not have a nucleus.

Cells without a nucleus are called prokaryotic cells. They are considered to be very primitive. Their DNA floats freely in their cytoplasm.

Osmosis: Movement In and Out of Cells

The cell membrane that surrounds an animal cell is semipermeable. Likewise, the cell walls of plants are also semipermeable.

"Semipermeable" means the boundary has a structure that keeps out some substances, but lets other substances pass. Only molecules of only certain sizes can cross a semipermeable boundary. It blocks out all other molecules.

The movement of molecules across a semipermeable membrane or border is called "osmosis." Osmosis is a kind of passive transport.

A cell does not does not use any energy for osmosis to occur. Water, some other liquid, or substances within those liquids move across the boundary selectively.

Osmosis causes molecules to move from an area of low concentration to an area of high concentration.

It is one of the ways in which plant roots take up water and nutrients from the soil. It is also how substances move from body cells into the bloodstream.

Tissues and Organs

Plants, animals, and some other organisms contain many cells. In these multicellular organisms, groups of similar cells form tissues. Each type of tissue has a particular function. In animals, one type of tissue makes up skin and another type of tissue makes up bones. Muscle cells group together to make muscle

Amoebas

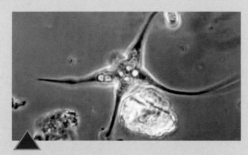

An amoeba is one of the most common simple life forms.

The amoeba is a single-celled organism that lives in water or in wet soil. It moves and changes shape by pushing out some of its cytoplasm to create a pseudopod (false foot). The pseudopod also helps the amoeba eat. An amoeba does not have a mouth. Instead, it wraps its pseudopods around the food. Chemicals ooze out of the cytoplasm to break down food. An amoeba takes in oxygen from water though its outer covering. It gives off waste in the same way. Biologists once thought the amoeba was an animal. We now classify amoebas as organisms called protozoans. Some amoebas can cause serious diseases in humans.

tissue. In plants, similar cells join to make up the tissue that forms roots, stems, and leaves.

Different kinds of tissues form organs, such as the stomach. Different kinds of organs often work together in a system. The mouth, stomach, and intestines are

Pronunciation Key:

amoeba (*ah-ME-bah*)
eukaryotic (*you-CARE-ee-AH-tick*)
nucleus (*NEW-klee-us*)
prokaryotic (*pro-CARE-ee-AH-tick*)

all important organs that help form the digestive system.

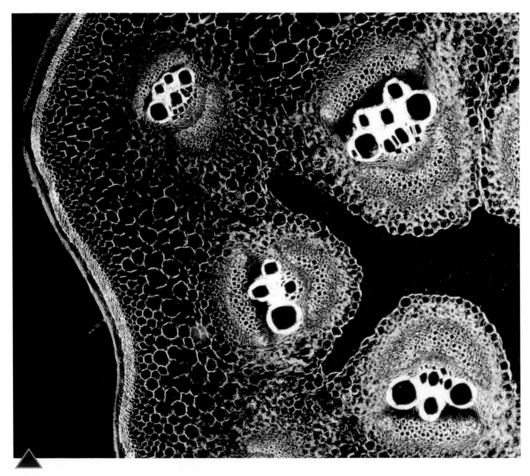

Individual tissue elements are visible under a microscope.

8

2 Animal Cells

All animal cells have an outer covering called the cell membrane. The cytoplasm is enclosed in the membrane much like a gel in a plastic bag. The flexible cell membrane enables animal cells to take on different shapes. The shape of an animal cell depends on its function.

Although cells can have many different shapes and sizes, they contain similar structures.

▼

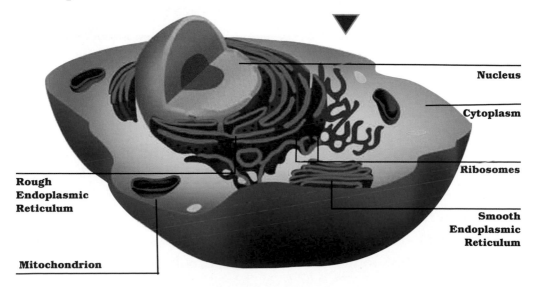

Nucleus

Cytoplasm

Ribosomes

Rough Endoplasmic Reticulum

Smooth Endoplasmic Reticulum

Mitochondrion

Cytoskeleton

Many animals have skeletons made of bone that support tissues and organs and help give the animal its shape. A cell does not have bones. It can have a distinct shape, however. A cell gets its shape from its cytoskeleton. The cytoskeleton is made of tiny fibers and microtubules that run throughout the cell. It helps one-celled animals move. In other animals, the cytoskeleton forms a sort of transportation system to move around substances within or between cells.

Plants also have cytoskeletons. Plant cells cannot move around. The plant cell's cytoskelekton helps give support to the cell.

Biologists (scientists who study living organisms) learned about cytoskeletons and other cell structures by studying cells using an electron microscope. An electron microscope uses electrons instead of light rays to create an image. The two main types of these microscopes cause electrons to travel through or bounce off the material being studied.

Skin Cells

Skin cells form the largest organ of the body. Our skin protects and cushions our muscles and internal organs. It produces hair and sweat. It grows in three main layers.

Skin cells can have many shapes, according to where they are found. They can be flat, cube-shaped, or long— like a rectangle or column. The outermost layer of skin is called the epidermis. It is the part we see. The surface of the epidermis is made of dead skin cells. They make the skin waterproof. Skin cells in the

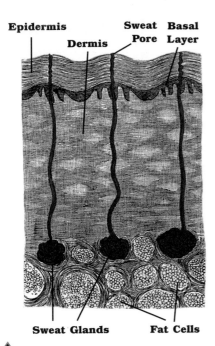

Epidermis   Sweat   Basal
        Dermis   Pore   Layer

Sweat Glands   Fat Cells

A cross-sectional view of skin
reveals structures within the layers.

lower part of the epidermis
make a tough substance called
keratin. Our hair, fingernails,
and toenails are made of
keratin. Feathers, fur, hooves,
and scales of other animals
are also made of keratin.

The bottom layer of the
epidermis is called the basal
layer. Basal cells make new
skin cells. The new skin cells
slowly move up to replace the
dead, outer layer of skin cells
that wears away every day.

Melanin

*Melanin (dark areas) is
a natural skin pigment.*

Specialized skin cells called
melanocytes make a pigment
called melanin. (A pigment
gives color to an object.)
Melanin is dark brown. It
provides color to hair, eyes,
feathers, and fur. The more
melanin produced, the darker
the tissue of the animal. For
instance, the irises of brown
eyes contain lots of melanin.
Light eye color indicates a
lack of melanin. And rather
than a sign of health, tanning
actually signals damaged skin.
Overexposure to the
ultraviolet radiation in
sunlight stimulates the
melanocytes to produce
extra melanin pigment.

Two layers—the dermis and hypodermis—lie below the epidermis. Ninety percent of the dermis in a cow is made of tough connective tissue called collagen. This is the skin layer that we dry and tan to make leather.

Muscle Cells

There are three types of muscle cells: skeletal (striated), smooth, or heart (cardiac). Each kind of muscle cell has a slightly different shape. Skeletal muscle cells are long and thin and are striated (striped). They have more than one nucleus.

These cells make up the muscles that attach to bones. All skeletal muscles work in pairs to contract (shorten), which allows a body to move. For instance, when an animal's brain tells its legs to run, the skeletal muscles contract, causing the bones in the legs to move.

All skeletal muscles work in pairs. When the brain signals a muscle to contract, an opposing muscle must relax at the same time.

Smooth muscle cells are not as long as skeletal muscle cells. They are not striated, and they only have one nucleus. Smooth muscles make up the walls of blood vessels, intestines, and other other internal organs. Smooth muscle works automatically. An animal cannot control smooth muscle movement.

Cardiac muscle cells are only found in the heart. They only have one nucleus. Heart muscle cells are striped and look very similar to skeletal muscle cells.

Cardiac cells, however, also have special disks that allow them to communicate with one another. These disks enable all of the cardiac muscle cells to work as a single unit. An animals does not control the contractions of its cardiac muscle cells. They work automatically to make the heart pump.

Nerve Cells

Fibers of two different lengths stretch out from the main nerve cell body, or neuron. These fibers help create a communication network within the body. The shorter fibers, called dendrites, carry nerve signals to the cell body.

Each neuron also has one longer fiber, called an axon. The axon relays the nerve cell signal to the dendrites of another neuron.

Sensory nerve cells detect what is going on outside an animal's body. The animal then reacts to the stimulus.

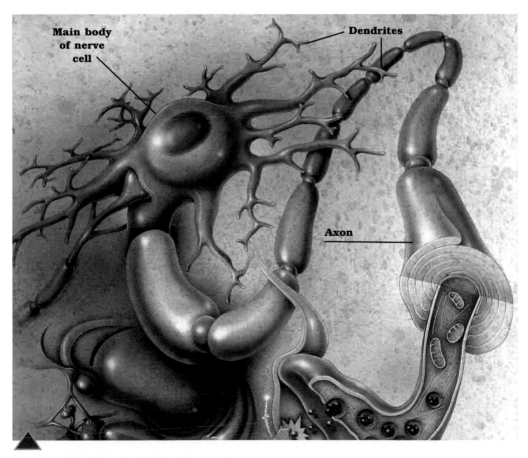

Main body of nerve cell

Dendrites

Axon

Nerve cells carry messages to and from the brain.

Sickle Cell Anemia

Cells must be the right shape in order to do their job. Sickle cell anemia occurs when red blood cells (RBCs) form in the wrong shape. Instead of being round and flexible, these RBCs are stiff and curved, like a sickle. The malformed RBCs cannot squeeze through small blood vessels. Unlike normal RBCs, they cannot carry oxygen around the body or remove the body's waste products.

Sickle cell anemia is an inherited disease. It often occurs in people whose ancestors are from Africa or the Middle East. People with sickle cell disease suffer from constant pain in bones, muscles, and organs. It zaps their energy, and they easily catch infections. There is no cure. To learn more, visit this Web site: *www.ygyh.org/sickle/whatisit.htm*

For example, an animal's senses of smell, hearing, and sight keep it safe. If a deer smells a predator, nerves carry the scent to its brain. The deer runs to safety.

A reflex, meanwhile, is an automatic nervous response that does not involve sending the nerve's message all the way to the animal's brain. If you touch something hot, you instantly withdraw your hand. In this case, the nerve signal, or impulse, only gets as far as your spinal cord before another impulse is on its way back to your arm muscles to contract and escape danger.

Blood Cells

Blood consists of several types of cells. Each looks very different from another, and each does a specific job. The main types of blood cells are red blood cells (RBCs) and white blood cells (WBCs).

Red blood cells are smooth and round, like tires. Mature RBCs are the only body cells without a nucleus. Red blood cells pick up oxygen from your lungs and carry it to all the cells in your body. They also carry carbon dioxide—a waste product given off by cells—back to your lungs. Red blood cells are flexible enough to squeeze through even the tiniest blood vessels.

White blood cells are large cells of several types that help form your disease-fighting immune system. They patrol the bloodstream and attack germs and viruses and fight infections. Other types of WBCs respond to an injury. The many different kinds of WBCs work together to repair the damaged tissues.

The blood also contains tiny disk-shaped structures, called platelets, that help blood clot.

Red blood cells are the most numerous type of blood cell.

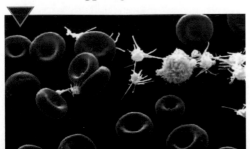

Altitude and Red Blood Cells

Animals and people who live at high altitudes have more RBCs than people who live at sea level. The higher the altitude, the less oxygen in the air. The extra RBCs allow these people and animals to get enough oxygen to their tissues. You must live at the higher altitude for several weeks to boost your RBC count.

Pronunciation Key:

cilia (*SI-lee-ah*)
collagen (*KAH-leh-jin*)
cytoplasm (*SIGH-toe-plaz-em*)
cytoskeleton (*SIGH-toe-skel-e-ton*)
flagellae (*FLA-je-lay*)
keratin (*CARE-uh-tin*)
melanocytes (*meh-LA-no-sites*)
mitochondrion (*MY-toe-KON-dre-on*)
organelle (*OR-guh-NELL*)
striated (*STRY-ay-tid*)

15

3 Plant Cells

Like animals, all plants are made of cells. The bigger the plant, the more cells it contains. A giant redwood tree has trillions of cells. Some simple plants, called algae, may only have one cell.

Under a microscope, plant cells look slightly different from animal cells. Plants have stiff cell walls instead of flexible cell membranes. Cell walls are made of a tough substance called cellulose.

Most plant cells are square or rectangular. Just as animal cells can be compared to a gel inside a plastic bag, plant cells are like a gel inside a cardboard box.

Plant cells often contain a large, tank-like structure called a vacuole. The vacuole stores food and water. A plant droops when its vacuoles are empty. Watering a plant fills up the vacuoles again. The leaves of the plant look plump and perky.

The cells of green plants also contain organelles called chloroplasts. They produce chlorophyll. Chlorophyll is a green-colored pigment that helps plants make their own food. Chlorophyll takes in energy from sunlight. The plant uses this energy along with water and carbon dioxide to make food. This process is called photosynthesis.

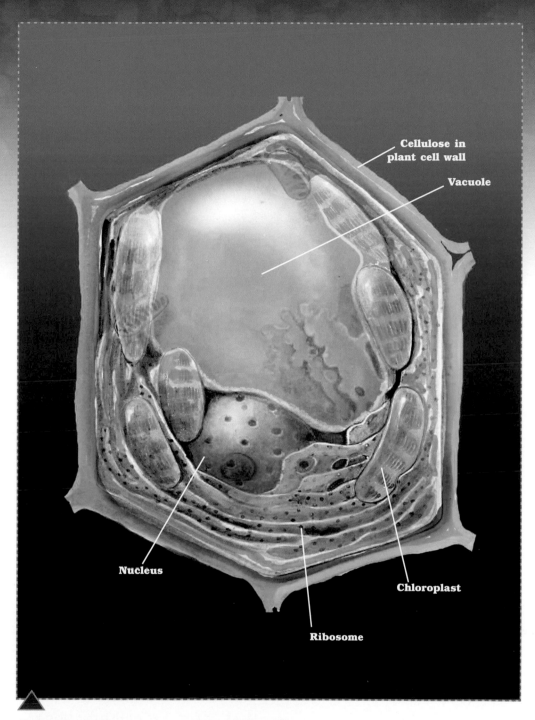

Cellulose in
plant cell wall

Vacuole

Nucleus

Chloroplast

Ribosome

Cellulose helps support plant cell walls.
Vacuoles store water. Chloroplasts make
chlorophyll. Chlorophyll makes plants green.

17

The Meat-eating Venus Flytrap

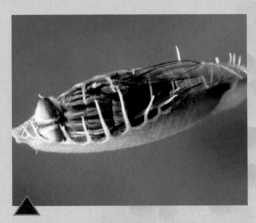

A fly is caught in the death grip of a Venus flytrap leaf.

Although they make their own energy, some plants appear to also eat animals, such as small insects. These "meat-eating" plants are called carnivorous plants. The strange-looking Venus flytrap is a carnivorous plant. It grows on the coastal plains of North and South Carolina. These plants normally grow in poor soil, so they developed a fascinating way to get the extra minerals they need. A Venus flytrap has specialized leaf structures that form traps. The edges of the traps bristle with needlelike spikes. The inside surface of the trap gives off a scent that lures insects. Tiny "hair triggers" on the open trap react when an insect lands. When an insect hits one of these hair triggers, the trap snaps shut to capture the insect. The large spikes act like prison bars to keep the creature inside. The plant then secretes powerful fluids that break down—or digest—the insect.

Plant cells have some parts that are similar to those in animal cells. Plant cells contain a nucleus with genes that direct the activities of the cell. Plant cells also have cytoplasm with organelles that carry out cell functions. Similar plant cells join together to form tissues, organs, and systems. Also, as with animals, plants contain several different types of cells.

Epidermal Cells

Epidermal cells form the protective outer layer of plant parts—just as epidermal cells form the skin of animals. Epidermal cells cover the roots and protect the tip, or root cap, as it burrows deeper into the ground. Tiny hairs on some epidermal cells help roots take up (absorb) water and minerals from the soil. Epidermal cells also form the outer layer of tree trunks and plant stems. Epidermal cells cover leaves and fruit.

The epidermis on the underside of leaves has tiny openings called stomata. These openings allow carbon dioxide to enter the leaf. Plants also give off oxygen through the stomata. Special guard cells nearby change in size to control the opening and closing of the stomata.

A close-up of plant epidermal cells

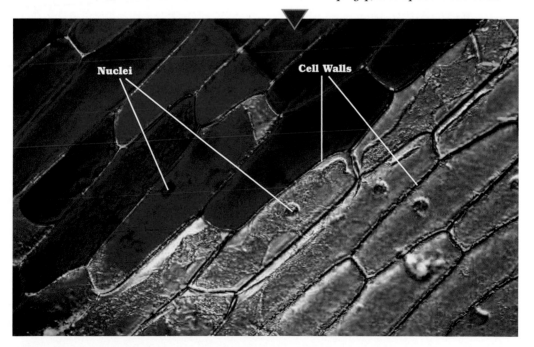

Nuclei

Cell Walls

Ground Tissue

Ground tissue is a general name for the tissues that make up a plant. The ground tissues in roots, leaves, and stems store food and water in their large vacuoles. Photosynthesis also occurs within the ground tissue.

Some ground tissue cells contain cellulose. This rigid material helps support stems and forms the hard shells of nuts. Oddly enough, the cells that contain cellulose must mature, die, and harden in order to do their job.

Vascular Tissue

The vascular system of a plant consists of a network of tubes that run throughout the plant. This network transports water, minerals, and the nutrients made through photosynthesis around the entire plant.

Tubes called the xylem and phloem form the network. It functions as a sort of plumbing system for the plant.

🔑 Pronunciation Key:

balsa (*BAHL-sah*)
cellulose (*SELL-ya-loz*)
chlorophyll (*KLOR-oh-fil*)
chloroplast (*KLOR-oh-plast*)
lignin (*lig-nen*)
osmosis (*az-MOH-ses*)
phloem (*FLO-im*)
photosynthesis
(*foh-toe-SIN-thuh-sis*)
stomata (*STO-mah-tah*)
vacuole (*VA-kyu-WOL*)
xylem (*ZEYE-lem*)

Xylem brings water and minerals up from the roots. Cells in the xylem must be dead and hollow to do their job correctly.

Phloem carries food from its production site in the leaves to different sites in the plant.

The main cells of phloem contain many holes, called pores. These cells resemble a strainer, or sieve. They are called sieve cells. Sieve cells look empty but are alive.

Softwoods and Hardwoods

The lumber used for building everything from desks to houses comes mainly from dead xylem tissue of trees. Two basic types of wood are used for construction—hardwood and softwood. Trees that produce hardwood grow much more slowly than those that produce softwood. Builders often put hardwood floors in houses. Oak, maple, and hickory are hardwoods. They are tough and can take the pounding of heavy use over a long period of time. Pine and fir are softwoods. They are easier to saw and hammer. Balsa is the softest wood in the world—yet it is technically considered a hardwood! The growth rate and thickness of the trees' cell walls determines the hardness of the wood. Substances such as cellulose and lignin make the cell walls stiff. Trees with the thickest cell walls produce the hardest wood.

An oak is a hardwood tree.

4 How Cells Reproduce

Cell Division

Every minute of your life, your body creates about two hundred million new cells. These new cells help replace damaged or worn-out cells. Cells multiply by dividing. They do this in several stages. A cell's "resting" stage is called interphase. Cells never really "rest," however. They are always busy keeping your body alive. Other stages of cell division include prophase, metaphase, anaphase, and telophase.

Every living organism will eventually die. So, in order to ensure that Earth has a fresh and steady supply of plants and animals, they must reproduce. Their offspring must also reproduce—or life on our planet would someday disappear. Likewise, every cell has a limited life span. For instance, your body cells are constantly dying and being replaced.

Cells in animals and plants either make up some part of the main body of that organism or are sex cells. Plant and animals cells that are not sex cells are called somatic cells. All somatic cells contain a complete copy of that organism's DNA. When somatic cells reproduce, they make exact copies of themselves. They replace or repair nearby tissues.

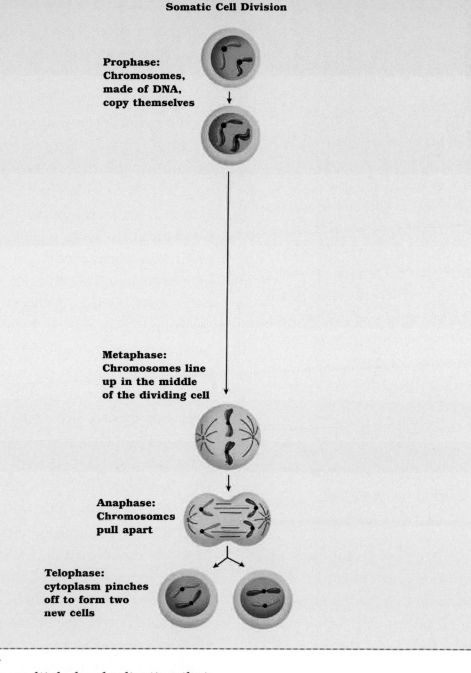

MITOSIS
Somatic Cell Division

Prophase:
Chromosomes,
made of DNA,
copy themselves

Metaphase:
Chromosomes line
up in the middle
of the dividing cell

Anaphase:
Chromosomes
pull apart

Telophase:
cytoplasm pinches
off to form two
new cells

Cells multiply by duplicating their
genetic material and splitting in two.
This process is called mitosis.

How Many Chromosomes?

Chromosome numbers in a plant or animal differ according to the species of that plant or animal. The number of chromosomes for an organism does not depend on the size or complexity of the plant or animal. A human being has 46 chromosomes (23 pairs) in each of his or her body cells. A dog has 78 chromosomes (39 pairs) in its body cells. A pea plant has 14 chromosomes, while a sunflower has 34—but one species of fern (a very simple kind of plant) has more than 1,200 chromosomes!

Sex cells are the eggs of females and sperm in males. They each contain only half the amount of DNA as somatic cells. Sex cells do not multiply to replace or repair other sex cells. Each sex cell of an organism is unique.

Single-celled organisms, including amoebas and bacteria, also reproduce. It is a relatively simple process. Single-celled organisms can create a copy of themselves by simply splitting in half or by growing a bud. The bud gets to a certain size and then pinches off to form a new organism. Either way, the new organism has exactly the same DNA as the "parent" organism from which it came.

Bacteria can also exchange genetic information during a process called conjugation. It does not involve sex cells.

Mitotic Cell Division

The process of creating a new body cell is called mitosis. It produces two somatic cells that are exactly alike. Each has a complete copy of the genes for that organism.

Genes control the traits of all living organisms. A gene is made of a chemical called DNA (deoxyribonucleic acid). Genes are found in the cell's nucleus.

Unless that cell is actively dividing, the genetic material of a cell exists as chromatin. Chromatin is a loosely organized material. It does not form into recognizable shapes until cell division is underway.

Once cell division begins, the chromatin forms thread-like structures called chromosomes. In eukaryotic cells, the chromosomes form in the nucleus. They make copies of themselves and form pairs called sister chromatids. A structure called a centromere attaches the pair of sister chromatids together. Each pair of chromosomes looks like an "X" when viewed through a microscope.

Mitosis has four phases. It begins with prophase. During prophase, the chromosomes form and duplicate themselves. The doubled chromosomes get thicker and shorter. The nuclear membrane slowly disappears. In the cytoplasm, tiny structures called centrioles move to either end of the cell.

Thin fibers form and appear to link, spanning the cell between the centrioles. They create a structure called a spindle.

The next phase is called metaphase. The sister chromatids line up with their centromeres in the middle of the spindle, called the "equator." They arrange themselves so that one copy of each chromatid is on an opposite side of the equator. Metaphase ends as the centromeres split apart.

In anaphase, the third stage, the sister chromatids separate. Each travels to opposite poles of the spindle.

Telophase is the last stage of mitosis. The spindle disappears. The nuclear membrane reforms. Inside each new nucleus, the chromosomes lose their distinct shape. The cytoplasm pinches off into two separate cells. During telophase in plants, new cell walls grow between the nuclei to produce two cells. Cells produced by mitosis are called daughter cells.

Stem Cells

Stem cells are amazing cells. They have the ability to develop into any kind of cell. Embryonic stem cells are the first cells that develop after a sperm fertilizes an egg. As the fertilized egg cell divides, it forms a hollow ball. In humans, this ball is called a blastocyst. In less complicated organisms, this ball is called a blastula. A special layer of stem cells within the blastocyst can develop into any kind of cell, from a brain cell to a muscle cell to a skin cell.

Stem cells also grow within some tissues, such as bone marrow and skeletal muscles.

They are the cells that help keep the body healthy. For example—and depending upon what the body needs—stem cells in the bone marrow could become red cells that carry oxygen. Or, these same stem cells could instead become white blood cells that fight disease.

Researchers believe that embryonic stem cells could help treat or even cure many serious diseases. Many people object to stem cell research. They do not like the fact that the embryo must be destroyed in order to harvest its stem cells for research.

Sex Cells from Meiosis

Meiosis is a special kind of cell division that only occurs in organisms that reproduce sexually. Meiosis produces sex cells, or gametes. In animals, male sex cells are called sperm and female sex cells are called eggs, or ova. In plants, female sex cells are also called ova, but male sex cells are called pollen.

The main difference between body cells and sex cells are the

MEIOSIS

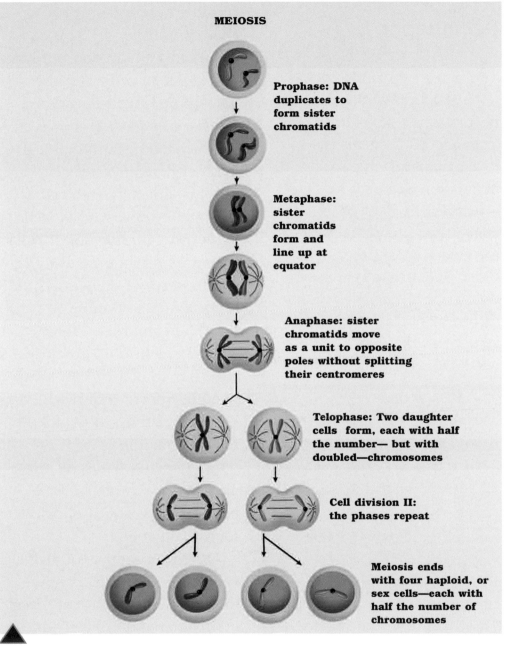

Prophase: DNA
duplicates to
form sister
chromatids

Metaphase:
sister
chromatids
form and
line up at
equator

Anaphase: sister
chromatids move
as a unit to opposite
poles without splitting
their centromeres

Telophase: Two daughter
cells form, each with half
the number— but with
doubled—chromosomes

Cell division II:
the phases repeat

Meiosis ends
with four haploid, or
sex cells—each with
half the number of
chromosomes

*Meiotic cell division
produces sex cells.*

Pollination

There are two kinds of pollination. Self-pollination occurs when pollen from a stamen lands on the pistil of the same plant. Cross-pollination occurs when insects, birds, bats, other animals, or the wind carry the pollen to another plant. Most plants have structures that favor cross-pollination. Other plants have structures that work better for self-pollination.

Asexual Reproduction

Not all animals need sex cells to reproduce. For example, a flatworm called a planarian reproduces asexually. Its body divides into two sections. The new flatworms have the same chromosomes and genes as the original planarian.

number of chromosomes they contain.

Mitotic cell division produces two identical cells with the same pairs of chromosomes. Meiotic cell division, however, produces four, non-identical cells with a single set of chromosomes in each cell.

Special reproductive cells undergo a double set of cell divisions during meiosis. In the first set of divisions, the chromosomes double to form sister chromatids. These structures line up so close together that they can swap genetic information with each another. Such swaps are called crossing over. It is why offspring can look very similar to parents and to each other without sharing identical genes.

During anaphase of meiosis, the sister chromatids stay attached to each other. Their centromeres do not divide. The daughter cells that form contain half the number of chromosomes, but each is double stranded. These two cells contain unique sets of genes. The main difference between mitosis and meiosis now becomes clear. These two new cells undergo a second set of cell division phases.

This time, the chromosomes do not duplicate. Instead, the two cells divide into four new cells—each with only a half set of chromosomes.

How An Embryo Grows

As a male and female sex cell unite, they create one new cell with a complete set of chromosomal pairs. How do muscle, nerve, and skin cells develop from this one cell?

The brand-new cell created when the sperm and egg join begins dividing. The cells keep dividing over and over again. In a process that biologists do not yet fully understand, the cells begin to take on specialized jobs. They form groups of cells based on the jobs they do. In humans, for example, the cells eventually

Sex Cells and Gender

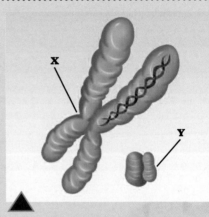

Sex-linked genes are located on the X and Y chromosomes.

Special chromosomes, called the X and Y chromosomes, determine the sex of human beings. Female eggs carry only the X chromosomes. Sperm may carry either an X or a Y chromosome. The father's sperm determines whether the baby is a boy or a girl. If the sperm carries a Y chromosome, the baby will be a boy (XY). If the sperm carries an X chromosome, the baby will be a girl (XX).

DNA's On-off Switch

Each somatic cell in an organism contains a complete copy of the genes for that organism. A cell in the leaf of a tree contains all the genes for every part of the tree. A skin cell in an animal contains all the genes for the animal's brain, bones, and blood. How does a skin cell know to act as a skin cell if it holds all the instructions for every other kind of cell?

The only DNA that gets "turned on" is the part of the DNA that the cell needs to function. If an organism's DNA were an instruction manual, skin cells would only turn to the pages about skin cells. Nerve cells would only read the instructions for nerve cells. This process is called gene regulation. Much research is still underway on this process.

become bone, skin, muscle, blood, nerve, or other types of body cells.

The cells form tissues, organs, and systems that work together to create a person. As old cells die, new cells created through mitosis keep that person healthy.

Alternation of Generations

In animals, a new cell formed when sperm and egg join keeps dividing and forming different tissues and organs—similar to the way in which human cells develop.

The process of making a new plant is somewhat different. It involves a series of steps called alternation of generations. Plants have two phases, the sporophyte phase and the gametophyte phase.

The sporophyte is the plant phase that people recognize as a particular plant. Oak trees, marigolds and other flowering plants, and pine trees are sporophytes. The sporophytes of flowering plants grow from seeds. The sporophytes of pine, spruce, and other plants that produce cones instead of flowers also grow from seeds.

The male and female stages of cone-bearing plants are both cones, but they do not look alike. The male cone is small and soft. The female cone has the familiar, hard cone shape.

Sporophytes produce spores by meiosis. In flowering plants, the female part of the plant is called the pistil. The male part of the flower is called the stamen.

🔑 Pronunciation Key:

chromatids (*KRO-meh-tids*)

chromosome (*KRO-meh-sohm*)

gametes (*GEAH-meets*)

gametophyte (*geah-MEE-toe-fite*)

meiosis (*my-OH-sis*)

mitosis (*my-TOE-sis*)

nucleus (*NEW-klee-us*)

ovule (*AHV-yule*)

sporophyte (*SPORE-oh-fite*)

Spores, in turn, produce gametophytes. Female gametophytes produce egg cells in structures called ovules. Male gametophytes produce pollen grains.

Gametophytes produce seeds. Insects or the wind carry pollen to the pistils. Pollen fertilizes the ovules. Ovules become seeds, from which sporophytes grow.

Gametophytes of flowering and cone-bearing plants live in the reproductive parts of the sporophytes. Most gametophytes are invisible to the naked eye. Mosses are about the only gametophytes we can see without using a microscope.

Cells From the Past

Paleontologists, scientists who study past life, use fossilized pollen grains to learn about prehistoric plants.

31

5 Cells as Factories

All cells are like tiny chemical factories. They must produce and regulate the chemicals needed to keep that organism alive and healthy.

Like any factory, a cell needs to receive a steady supply of raw materials to keep functioning. Chemicals move in and out of the cells through tiny openings.

Miniature structures within the cytoplasm make up the manufacturing equipment in cells. These structures are called organelles.

The organelles work together to help the cell produce what it needs. Proteins called hormones and enzymes are the main kinds of chemicals cells produce.

DNA and RNA

The cell nucleus controls how each cell functions. It contains the genes, which are made of DNA. The DNA is like a blueprint that describes how to make a completely new cell. It also tells cells exactly how to assemble the different proteins needed to create new cells.

Another chemical, called RNA, helps make cellular proteins. Some proteins repair the cell and keep it healthy. Other proteins are enzymes that start or speed up chemical reactions. Hormones

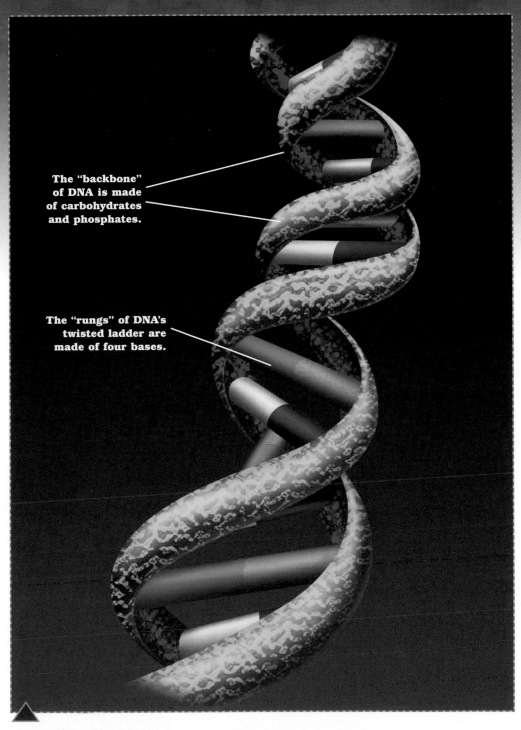

The "backbone" of DNA is made of carbohydrates and phosphates.

The "rungs" of DNA's twisted ladder are made of four bases.

The DNA molecule is shaped like a ladder twisted like a corkscrew. This shape is called a double helix.

are proteins that regulate many of the metabolic functions of plants and animals.

Proteins are made of chemicals called amino acids. Amino acids are the building blocks ("Legos") of proteins. There are twenty amino acids.

The nucleus often has one or more structures called nucleoli. Each nucleolus contains RNA. This chemical is very similar to DNA, but contains a base called uracil in place of thymine.

RNA carries the codes for cellular proteins. The cell may use the protein directly. It may also send the protein into the bloodstream for use elsewhere in the body.

Ribosomes

Organelles called ribosomes can "read" the RNA strand to manufacture the proteins. Ribosomes are tiny, dark granules. They can be freely scattered throughout the cytoplasm. Ribosomes can also be found on an organelle called the rough endoplasmic reticulum (ER).

There are two types of ER— smooth ER and rough ER. Both kinds serve as a tubular communication system between a cell's nucleus, its cytoplasm, and its outer boundary. A cell may have more than one rough or smooth endoplasmic reticulum organelle.

Smooth ER makes lipids (fats) for cell membranes. In liver cells, smooth ER helps filter out cell poisons. In brain and muscle cells, smooth ER stores the mineral calcium.

Ribosomes give rough ER its bumpy appearance. Proteins made by the rough ER are sent out of the cell. Proteins made by the free-floating ribosomes in the cytoplasm are used by the cell itself.

A cell protein is stored in a bubble-like organelle called a vesicle. Protein for transport goes to another organelle, called the Golgi apparatus.

An artistic illustration shows the inner structure of rough ER.

Golgi Apparatus

The Golgi apparatus (or body) is another part of a cell's transport and storage system. The Golgi apparatus "labels" the cell products it stores. It also determines where the cell products should be sent.

The Golgi bodies also help produce organelles called lysosomes. These are sacs that contain powerful digestive enzymes. Lysosomes are like little stomachs inside animals cells. They help the cell digest food molecles and other large molecules.

White blood cells contain many lysosomes to help break down ("digest") germs. When a cell dies, its lysosomes digest the cell parts.

35

Tubes and Pores

Special cells called phloem transport food around a plant. Phloem cells have a tube-like structure. They act somewhat like the plumbing system in your home. The phloem allows the flow of water and nutrients to all parts of the plant.

Photosynthesis in plants produces waste gases— water vapor and oxygen. These gases are released through tiny pores, called stomata, found mostly on the undersides of leaves. Escaping water vapor cools the leaves—a process called transpiration. Oxygen given off is breathed in by animals.

Vacuoles

All animal and plant cells have storage areas for liquids, called vacuoles. Plant cell vacuoles are much larger than those in animal cells. Vacuoles can also store waste products.

Mitochondria

Mitochondria are the powerhouses of the cell. A cell that needs a lot energy has a lot of mitochondria. Muscle cells, for example, can have thousands of mitochondria. They help provide energy for an athelete's trained muscles. Mitochondria also have their own unique DNA.

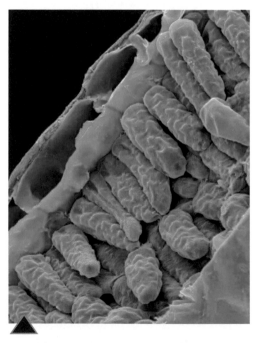

An electron micrograph shows the detailed structure of chloroplasts.

Materials for the Cells

Animal and plant cells use the raw materials from food for energy and to make the different proteins needed by the organism.

Green plants use special organelles, called chloroplasts, to produce their own food. Chloroplasts are the sites where photosynthesis occurs. They are found mainly in the leaf cells of green plants.

Chloroplasts contain a green pigment called chlorophyll. The chlorophyll uses sunlight—along with water and carbon dioxide gas —to make a sugar, which the plant uses for food.

Animals must break down, or digest, their food to get energy from it. Digestion breaks down the food into molecules usable by cells.

Fats are broken down into fatty acids. Proteins are broken down into amino acids. Carbohydrates are tuned into simple sugars.

Millions of Stomata

Stomata make plant leaves very efficient at taking in carbon dioxide and giving off water vapor and oxygen. For instance, one leaf of a sunflower plant contains about two million stomata. Nearly all of these are on the underside of the leaf.

These substances pass through the cell membrane. Inside the cell, the mitochondria produce energy from the food substances.

The RNA and ribosomes assemble the amino acids into new proteins. And so the cycle repeats itself.

Bad Genes

A cancer is marked by the uncontrolled growth of cells. For example, normal body cells divide only when they need replacing or repair. Cancer cells have somehow lost that control. They divide

Parasites Are Not Good to Hosts

A parasite is an organism that gets its nourishment from another organism, called a host. For example, plants that lack chloroplasts must find another way to get the nutrients they need. Mistletoe is a partially parasitic plant. It makes some of its own food, but still needs a host tree.

wildly, often overtaking most of the normal cells in a tissue.

The cells in healthy tissues have a steady rate of death and renewal. Rapidly dividing cancerous cells simply keep multiplying. The large number of cancerous cells created can soon become a mass of cells called a tumor. A cancerous tumor can contain millions or even billions of cells.

Researchers have many theories about why cells become cancerous.

Sometimes, it is a genetic problem. The genes that tell a cell when to start and stop dividing stop working. They no longer send the signals that control cell division.

Cancer can develop in any body tissue or organ, including blood, breast, skin, lungs, muscles, and liver. Cancerous cells can also break loose from where they first grow. The cancer cells travel to other parts of the body through the blood or lymph systems, for instance. Breast cancer cells can travel to bones or the brain, where they may form a new tumor.

A cancer may develop if a few genes "go bad." Their base-pair alignments may change for some reason. This is called a mutation.

The mutation could cause the cell to assemble the wrong protein. If the protein controls cell division, the change may lead to cancer.

Researchers have identified many things that may cause

Sometimes, a cell's DNA mutates for no real reason at all. This actually happens on a daily basis, but most of the time the mutation does no harm. The cell either corrects itself or dies off. It is only when damaged cells do not get repaired or die that the tissues with the mutated cells could become cancerous.

Some people inherit DNA that is "pre-programmed" to mutate and develop into diseases such as cancer.

mutations. Repeated exposure to certain chemicals, such as those in cigarette smoke, can cause mutations in a cell's DNA. Overexposure to ultraviolet radiation from the Sun over many years can also damage DNA.

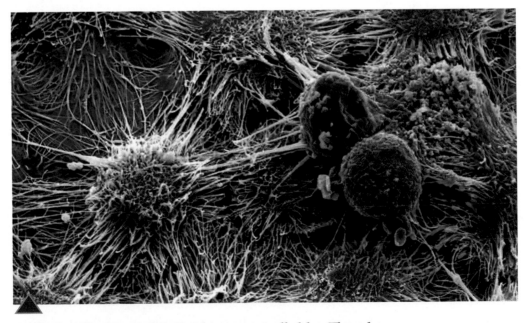

Cancer cells (in pink) *divide uncontrollably. They have a different appearance from normal tissue cells.*

Treating Cancer

Doctors use a variety of methods for treating cancer. Cancerous tissue can be surgically removed. Powerful drugs can kill cancer cells. Radiation treatments can also kill cancer cells.

Many of these treatments are very hard on the patients, however. Researchers are constantly looking for new and better ways to treat cancer. They also seek to prevent it from returning.

New breakthroughs in cancer research includes drugs that target only cancer cells. Other researchers study different ways of delivering those drugs. They are developing tiny robots that carry cancer drugs directly to the cancer cells. Other researchers study how a patient's genes may have been involved in the growth of that cancer. Doctors hope that someday they will find ways to treat the genetic causes of cancer.

Smoking is one way to increase your odds of getting lung cancer.

Cells and History

Our knowledge of cells and how they work has come a long way. More than four hundred years ago, English scientist Robert Hooke first coined the word "cell" to describe what he saw with his crude microscope. Hooke was examining a thin piece of cork bark. He noted that what he saw was "all perforated and porous, much like a Honey-comb, but that the pores of it were not regular. . . . these pores, or cells, . . . were indeed the first microscopical pores I ever saw, and perhaps, that were ever seen."

Hooke wrote about his discovery and drew pictures of his findings for an illustrated book called *Micrographia*, published in 1665.

Robert Hooke drew this image of cork cells to illustrate their unique structure.

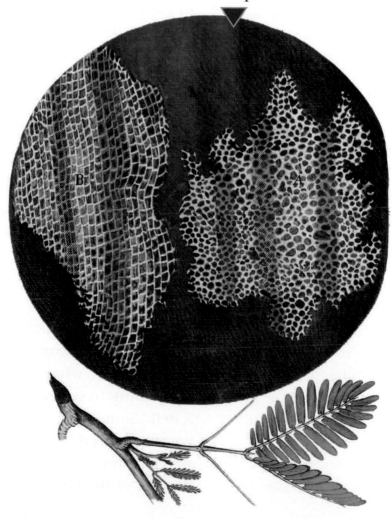

About twenty years later, Anton van Leeuwenhoek also used a microscope to study everyday objects. He viewed swamp water, blood, plant matter, and other materials with his microscope.

He even decided to scrape his teeth and looked at that matter with his microscope. (People did not regularly brush their teeth in the seventeenth century.)

To his surprise, he saw tiny organisms wriggling around in his tooth scum. He called them "animalcules."

Leeuwenhoek discovered or described many other cells, including red blood cells, sperm cells, and bacteria.

These two masters of the earliest microscopes paved the way for future generations of biologists. Still, they could not have predicted the enormous contributions that microscopes have made to scientific investigations.

As the centuries passed, inventors improved upon the methods used to grind lenses for the microscopes.

With the new lenses and better designs, microscopes became important tools for learning more about cell structure and function. By the mid-twentieth century, researchers were finally able to view cells using an electron microscope. Researchers, doctors, and other scientists could now see the exact structures of the incredible array of cell organelles. The next step was to figure out what each did.

In the last half-century or so, our understanding of how cells look and function has increased dramatically. We know the processes that cells use to communicate, create proteins, and duplicate themselves. Researchers can often identify what caused something to go wrong with a cell. Sometimes, they can correct such defects. Even so, we have not unlocked all the secrets of the cells.

Microbiology and Related Careers

Microbiologists are scientists who specialize in studying organisms that can only be seen with microscopes. They examine organisms such as bacteria and viruses. Microbiologists can identify different organisms. They try to determine how each causes animal diseases. They also study organisms that infect plants.

Many microbiologists work in hospitals or research laboratories. Others work for companies that develop and manufacture drugs, pesticides, and other biochemicals.

It takes many years of schooling to become a microbiologist. After high school, microbiologists must take advanced classes in biology, chemistry, and other sciences. Microbiologists often earn a master's (M.S.) or doctorate degree (Ph.D.).

Microbiologists help protect public health by analyzing food and water samples to detect any disease-causing microorganisms. Others work to prevent or control epidemics of infectious diseases. They are called epidemiologists. Those who specialize in the study of viruses are called virologists. Immunologists are doctors who study how the body's immune cells work.

A microbiologist may use an electron microscope to study microorganisms. Electron microscopes can magnify objects many more thousands of times than an ordinary light microscope.

43

Glossary

amino acids the "building blocks," or basic units, of proteins

amoeba a single-celled freshwater or marine organism with no permanent shape that moves using pseudopods

axon the long arm of a nerve cell that sends out signals

body cell any cell that contains a full set of chromosomes for that animal or plant

cancer a disease marked by cells that undergo continuous, uncontrollable cell division

carbon dioxide a gas in air that plants use for making food

cellulose a plant material that helps make cell walls rigid

chlorophyll a chemical produced by plants to capture the energy in sunlight

chloroplast a chlorophyll-containing organelle found in the cells of plants and a few primitive organisms

chromatid a copy of a chromosome

chromosome a strand of material that forms in the nucleus during cell division

collagen a fibrous material that adds support to connective tissues

cytoplasm a gel-like substance that makes up the main body of a cell

cytoskeleton a system of fibers and microtubules that helps support a cell and aids in its activities

dendrite a shorter extension of a nerve cell that receives signals

diffusion the flow of a fluid from an area of high particle concentration to an area of lower concentration

digestion the breaking down of food into simple chemicals

DNA (deoxyribonucleic acid) the chemical that makes up genes

endoplasmic reticulum (ER) a cell organelle consisting of a network of tubes and involved in protein manufacture and cell transport

eukaryotic referring to a plant or animal whose cells have nuclei

gametophyte a life stage of a plant when it produces sex cells

genes the basic units of heredity

Golgi body (also called Golgi complex or Golgi apparatus) a cell organelle consisting of sacs that store and transport cell components

ground tissue a nonspecific term for plant tissue

lignin a supportive material that helps give plant cells rigidity

lipids fats

lysosome an organelle that contains powerful digestive enzymes

meiosis the type of cell division that produces eggs and sperm cells

melanin a dark pigment produced by skin cells called melanocytes

microscope an instrument with a series of lenses that help magnify very tiny objects and organisms

mitochondrion the organelle that makes energy for the cell

mitosis the type of cell division that creates two identical cells

neuron a nerve cell

nucleus the command center of cell; controls all cell activities and functions, including cell division

organelle any of a number of cytoplasmic structures that perform a particular cell function

osmosis the selective flow of particles through a semipermeable membrane from an area of low concentration to an area of higher concentration

oxygen a gas given off by plants as part of normal cell respiration

photosynthesis the process by which plants make food using sunlight, carbon dioxide, and water

pistil the section of a flower that contains the female reproductive organs for that flower

pollen dust-like plant material that contains the male genetic information for that plant

prokaryotic referring to organisms whose cells lack nuclei

protein a chemical that helps carry out cell functions

ribosome an organelle that helps assemble cell proteins

root cap the tip of a root and site of active cell division (growth)

RNA (ribonucleic acid) a chemical found in a cell's nucleus that contains the genetic code for cell proteins

sex cell an egg or sperm cell, each of which contains only half the normal number of chromosomes for that organsim

sperm a male sex cell

sporophyte the spore-producing life stage of a plant

stamen the pollen-producing, male reproductive parts of a flower

stem cell an undifferentiated (immature) cell that can become any other kind of cell

stomata a pore (tiny opening) on a leaf that lets in carbon dioxide and gives off oxygen and water vapor

tissues groups of similar cells that work together to perform a particular function for an organism

ultraviolet rays invisible, damaging electromagnetic radiation that can increase the amount of dark pigment produced by melanocytes in the skin

For More Information

Books

Ball, Jacqueline A. *Cells*. Discovery Channel School Science (series). Gareth Stevens (2003)

Gillie, Oliver. *Sickle Cell Disease*. Just the Facts (series). Heinemann Library (2004)

Hall, Howard. *The Secrets of Kelp Forests: Life's Ebb and Flow in the Sea's Richest Habitat*. Jean-Michel Cousteau Presents (series). London Town Press (2007)

King, Katie. *Protists and Fungi*. Discovery Channel School Science (series). Gareth Stevens (2003)

Snedden, Robert. *Animals: Multicelled Life*. Cells and Life (series). Heinemann Library (2002)

Snedden, Robert. *Diversity of Life: From Single Cells to Multicellular Organisms*, Heinemann Library (2002)

Snedden, Robert and Andrew Solway. *Plants and Fungi: Multicelled Life*. Cells and Life (series). Heinemann Library (2002)

Spilsbury, Richard and Louise Spilsbury. *Green Plants: From Roots to Leaves*. Heinemann Library (2004)

Tesar, Jenny. *Stem Cells*. (Science on the Edge (series). Blackbirch Press (2003)

Yablonski, Judy. *Plant and Animal Cells: Understanding the Differences Between Plant and Animal Cells*. The Library of Cells (series). Rosen (2004)

Web Sites

www.eurekascience.com/ ICanDoThat/plant_cells.htm
Tour some plant cells with Cloe as your guide.

www.enchantedlearning.com/ subjects/animals/cell/
View a simple diagram of a typical animal cell and discover its many parts.

http://projects.edtech.sandi.net/miramesa/ Organelles/animal.html
Learn more about your favorite organelle.

www.eurekascience.com/ ICanDoThat/animal_cells.htm
Tour the amazing variety of animals cells with Cloe as your guide.

www.dnaftb.org/dnaftb/
Follow the links to learn more about genetics.

www.lif.icnet.uk/kids/cellsrus/ cellsrus.html
Take a lighthearted look at cell division.

http://health.howstuffworks.com/ muscle2.htm
Get an inside view of how muscle fibers slide past each other as they contract and relax.

www.johnkyrk.com/meiosis.html
Watch an animation of meiotic cell division.

Publisher's note to educators and parents: Our editors have carefully reviewed these Web sites to ensure that they are suitable for children. Many Web sites change frequently, however, and we cannot guarantee that a site's future contents will continue to meet our high standards of quality and educational value. Be advised that children should be closely supervised whenever they access the Internet.

Index